BLOOD SUGAR
HEALTHY MEALS

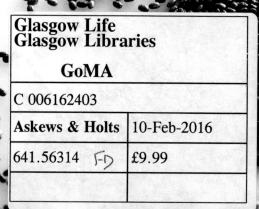

BLOOD SUGAR
HEALTHY MEALS

NEW
HOLLAND

MICHAEL MOORE

Introduction

From early and simple beginnings in the UK, Michael Moore started out in some of London's best restaurants, including the Cafe Royal and 45 Park Lane. Michael, whose love of food has inspired him to be on the world stage of international chefs who have a passion for great food and healthy living.

When Michael was diagnosed with diabetes, he was shocked. Having always led a fit, active and healthy lifestyle, Michael was more determined than ever to continue living his life as a diabetic without compromising on food.

After eight years of dealing with type 2 diabetes casually, Michael suffered a stroke and was forced to reevaluate how he was approaching food.

This is not a 'diet book', it is a collection of recipes developed over time to help keep diabetics, anyone who has suffered a stroke, or people who just want to eat good food while looking after your health, like Michael, on track without compromising on tasty foods.

No more does being a diabetic mean you are stuck in a gastronomic wilderness. You can have great food that's unexpected and exciting. It's all about keeping your blood sugar under control and balancing the ingredients to help you maintain good health.

Blood Sugar – Healthy Meals offers up to you a range of healthy and delicious dishes for breakfast, lunch, dinner and every snack in between.

Recipes

Rainy Day Hot Milk & Barley Porridge

SERVES 4

475ml (16fl oz) milk (2% fat)
2 tablespoons agave nectar
1 cinnamon quill
1 vanilla bean or teaspoon
    of vanilla essence
1 tablespoon sultanas
80g (3oz) rolled barley
    flakes
2 tablespoons sunflower
    seeds
2 tablespoons pepitas/
    pumpkin seeds
2 tablespoons flaked
    almonds
pinch ground nutmeg

1. In a medium-sized saucepan, heat 350ml (12fl oz) of milk with the agave nectar, cinnamon quill and the split vanilla bean or essence. Stir in the sultanas and the barley flakes and cook over a low heat for 10 minutes, stirring until thick and the barley is soft.
2. Meanwhile, in a preheated, non-stick frying pan cook together the sunflower, pepitas and flaked almonds until toasted and light brown. Allow to cool, then add to the porridge.
3. To serve, bring the remaining milk to the boil, whisking to make as much froth as possible (I use my coffee machine steamer to do this). Spoon the porridge into serving bowls, spoon some of the hot milk froth on top and dust with the ground nutmeg.

This is a lower GI version of traditional oat porridge, and is perfect for winter mornings. You'll find flaked barley in supermarkets and at food markets.

Crunchy Nut, Seed & Oat Clusters

MAKES APPROXIMATELY 40 SMALL CLUSTERS, SERVES 8 (5 PER PORTION)

120g (4oz) barley oat flakes
80g (3oz) nibbed almonds
60g (2oz) flax seeds/
linseeds
80g (3oz) unsalted peanuts
chopped
60g (2oz) hazelnuts
chopped
60g (2oz) pepitas/pumpkin
seeds
60g (2oz) sunflower seeds
60g (2oz) dried apricots,
chopped
60g (2oz) cornstarch/
cornflour
80g (3oz) agave nectar
1 teaspoon vanilla essence
80g (3oz) butter
3 large egg whites
1 tablespoon superfine/
caster sugar
fresh figs, natural yogurt and
milk, to serve

1. Preheat oven to 180°C (350°F). In a large mixing bowl combine all dry ingredients and mix well.
2. In a small saucepan melt together the agave nectar, vanilla essence and the butter. Pour over the dry ingredients and stir thoroughly, coating the dry ingredients as much as possible.
3. Using a whisk, vigorously beat the egg whites to a firm peak, adding the caster sugar at the end. Add the dry ingredients to the egg whites and mix well.
4. Place a sheet of baking parchment onto a baking tray, lightly spray with oil and place teaspoon-sized drops of the mixture at regular intervals, being careful not to let clusters touch each other.
5. Place in the oven and cook for 10 minutes, then reduce temperature to 150°C (300°F) and cook for a further 20 minutes. Remove clusters from the oven and allow to cool. The clusters should be lightly colored, dry and crunchy.
6. Store in a sealed container for up to 3 weeks. Serve with fresh figs, natural yogurt and milk.

This is my alternative to highly-sugared commercial cereals. My kids love them and can't tell the difference.

Poached Red Fruit Salad

SERVES 4

180ml (6fl oz) water
60g (2oz) agave nectar
1 small piece fresh ginger, grated
1 small bunch rhubarb
1 punnet strawberries
4 fresh black figs
60g (2oz) organic red or white quinoa
350ml (12fl oz) water
½ bunch fresh mint

1. Preheat oven to 180°C (360°F). In a small saucepan heat water and dissolve the agave nectar. Add grated ginger. Using a vegetable peeler, peel the rhubarb and cut into 3cm (1in) batons. Place the rhubarb into saucepan with agave liquid and cook on a low heat for approximately 2 minutes.
2. Trim the stalks from the strawberries. Cut the figs and strawberries in half and place them into an ovenproof dish. Pour the hot poached rhubarb and liquid over them. Place dish into oven for 5 minutes, remove and allow to cool in the liquid.
3. Place the quinoa in a small saucepan and cover with water. Bring to the boil and simmer for 15 minutes until plumped and tender, then drain and rinse under cold water.
4. Drain the liquid from the fruit and add it to the cooked quinoa with the finely chopped mint leaves.
5. Arrange the fruit on serving dishes and spoon the sweetened quinoa on the top.

Tip: Quinoa is a highly nutritious South American seed that can be substituted for most grains. It's available from health food stores and supermarkets.

Soft & Chewy Breakfast Bars

MAKES 12 BARS

120g (4oz) barley oat flakes
2 wheat breakfast cereal
    biscuits such as Vitabrits
    or Weet-Bix/Weetabix
60g (2oz) pepitas/pumpkin
    seeds
60g (2oz) pistachio nuts,
    chopped
60g (2oz) sunflower seeds
30g (1oz) white sesame
    seeds
30g (1oz) millet
30g (1oz) flax seeds/
    linseeds
30g (1oz) chia seeds
60g (2oz) dried cranberries,
    chopped
pinch dried ginger
pinch ground cinnamon
80g (3oz) butter
80g (3oz) agave nectar
80g (3oz) honey

1. Preheat oven to 180°C (360°F) degrees. In a large mixing bowl combine all dry ingredients, mix well.
2. In a small saucepan melt the butter, agave nectar and the honey. Pour this over the dry ingredients and stir, thoroughly coating the dry ingredients.
3. Line a baking tray with baking parchment and spray it lightly with oil. Pour mixture in and lightly flatten using the palm of your hand.
4. Place tray in oven and bake for 25 minutes, remove and allow to cool for 2 minutes in the tray. Using a large kitchen knife mark cut lines approximately 18 x 3cm (3 x 1in) wide. Place in refrigerator until set.
5. Once set, break or cut bars into pieces and store in an airtight container for up to 3 weeks.

Tip: Chia seeds, known as the Aztec 'super food' are one of the highest plant sources of Omega 3 fatty acids, as well as being rich in vitamins and fibre.

My kids love these bars—they don't take them to school because of the nuts, but they are easy to make for a weekend or after-school treat.

Toffee, Carrot, Honey & Nut Slice

MAKES 1 LARGE TRAY, APPROXIMATELY 12 SERVES

350g (12oz) fresh full cream ricotta cheese

2 tablespoons agave nectar

120ml (4fl oz) fresh milk (2% fat)

60g (2oz) butter

1 tablespoon vegetable oil

175g (6oz) bakers/self-raising flour

½ teaspoon baking soda/bicarbonate of soda

60g (2oz) ground almonds

3 large fresh eggs

175g (6oz) fresh carrot, grated

60g (2oz) walnuts, roughly chopped

60g (2oz) slithered almonds

60g (2oz) pistachio nuts, chopped

120g (4oz) crème fraîche for frosting, sweetened with a little agave nectar

confectioners'/icing sugar or cinnamon to dust

1. Preheat oven to 180°C (360°F). Using an electric mixer, beat the ricotta for 3 minutes on a high speed until very smooth.

2. In a small saucepan melt the agave nectar with the milk, butter and oil then allow to cool.

3. In a bowl, sift together the flour, bicarbonate of soda and the ground almonds.

4. Reduce the mixer speed to slow, then gradually add the eggs and the milk mixture. Add the ground almonds and flour and combine together, but do not over mix.

5. Add the grated carrots and the chopped walnuts, slithered almonds and the pistachio nuts. Stir and mix through.

6. Grease and line a large toffee tray with baking parchment and spread the mixture evenly into it. Bake in oven for 30 minutes until firm to touch, remove from the oven and allow to cool in the tray. Using a large knife score the cake into portions approximately 5cm (2in) square or to your liking. Spread some crème fraîche on the top or dust with cinnamon or a little confectioners' sugar.

Stone Ground Muesli Hot Cakes

SERVES 4-6

60g (2oz) self-raising flour
60g (2oz) stone ground
　　whole-wheat flour
¼ teaspoon baking soda/
　　bicarbonate of soda
40g (1.5oz) whole rolled
　　oats
2 tablespoons slivered
　　almond
1 tablespoon LSA (ground
　　linseeds, sunflower seeds
　　and almonds)
1 tablespoon agave syrup
2 eggs
250ml (8fl oz) low-fat milk
cooking spray

VANILLA YOGURT
250g (9oz) low-fat natural
　　yogurt
2 tablespoons agave syrup
1 vanilla bean

RASPBERRY CRUSH
1 punnet (150g/5oz)
　　raspberries
1 teaspoon agave syrup

1. Combine flours, baking soda, oats, almonds and LSA in a
   large bowl and make a well in the centre. In a separate
   bowl, whisk together the agave, eggs and milk. Pour this into
   the dry ingredients. Mix until combined. The batter should be
   the consistency of double cream. Set aside for 30 minutes.
2. Meanwhile, mix yogurt and agave syrup together. Scrape
   seeds from vanilla bean and stir into yogurt. Refrigerate until
   needed.
3. Place half the raspberries into a bowl with the agave and
   crush with a fork until broken down. Stir in remaining
   raspberries and set aside.
4. Heat a non-stick frying pan and spray with cooking spray.
   Ladle spoonfuls of pancake batter into pan and cook for
   about 1 minute, or until bubbles appear on the surface of the
   pancake. Turn over and cook a further 45–60 seconds. Turn
   onto a plate and repeat with remaining batter.
5. Serve pancakes with raspberry sauce and a spoonful of
   vanilla yogurt.

*These are filling and a much healthier way of
eating pancakes.*

Slow-Baked Turkish Dates & Peaches with Porridge

SERVES 4

2 ripe peaches, halved

4 fresh Turkish dates, seeds removed

1 tablespoon date honey sauce

40g (1.5oz) rolled oats

pinch of salt

625ml (1 pint) low-fat milk

1 tablespoon pumpkin seeds

1 tablespoon sunflower seeds

1 tablespoon linseeds

extra hot milk to serve

DATE HONEY SAUCE

8 dates, pitted and chopped

juice of ½ lemon

125ml (4fl oz) water

60ml (2fl oz) agave syrup

1. Preheat oven to 200°C (400°F).
2. Place peaches and dates into a roasting dish and drizzle over date honey sauce. Roast for 30 minutes or until fruit is soft and the sauce is a syrup. Set aside to cool.
3. Meanwhile, place oats and salt into a medium saucepan and add half the milk, set aside for 5–10 minutes to help soften the oats. Add remaining milk and cook over medium heat until it boils. Reduce heat to low and stir until soft and creamy, approximately 15 minutes.
4. Stir the seeds into the porridge, then serve with warmed peaches and dates and drizzle with extra syrup.

To make Date Honey Sauce:
1. Mash dates lightly with a fork. Place into a small saucepan with lemon juice, water and agave.

2. Cook, stirring over low heat, until the water has been absorbed and it has a thick consistency. Cool completely and store in the refrigerator in a sealed jar.

I only ever use a little of this sauce at a time.

Blueberry & Tofu Protein Shake

SERVES 4

90g (3oz) silken/soft tofu
85g (3oz) fresh or frozen
    blueberries
1 banana
1 tablespoon agave syrup
2 tablespoons unprocessed
    bran
2 egg whites (optional)
720ml (25fl oz) chilled low-
    fat milk
2 teaspoons chia seeds

1. Combine all ingredients except chia seeds into a blender
   and pulse until smooth. Stir in the chia seeds then serve
   immediately in large chilled glasses.
2. Garnish with some berries.

Chef's note: You can buy chia seeds from health food shops and
    many supermarkets.

Greek Yogurt Parfait Cups

SERVES 4

1 tablespoon unprocessed
   bran
300g (10oz) natural low-fat
   Greek yogurt
1 tablespoon quinoa flakes
100ml (3fl oz) grape juice or
   apple juice
240ml (8fl oz) water
1 red apple
1 tablespoon agave nectar
½ punnet fresh blueberries
½ punnet fresh raspberries

1. In a small bowl mix the bran, yogurt, quinoa flakes and grape juice, then place in the fridge.
2. In a small saucepan heat the agave nectar with water. Peel and deseed the apple then cut it into 8 wedges. Poach these apples over a simmering heat for 10 minutes until soft and tender. Add the blueberries and raspberries, remove from the heat and allow fruit to cool in the liquid.
3. Remove fruit from the saucepan using a slotted spoon and layer alternately with the yogurt mixture into serving glasses. Place in the fridge to cool before serving.

Tip: Quinoa is a highly nutritious South American seed that can be substituted for most grains. It's available from health food stores and supermarkets.

Dark Chocolate, Nut & Banana Thick Shake

SERVES 4

60g (2oz) dark chocolate
1 teaspoon agave nectar
1 tablespoon cocoa powder
    (unsweetened)
600ml (1 pint) almond milk
1 large ripe banana
1 tablespoon honey
120ml (4fl oz) natural yogurt
120ml (4fl oz) silken tofu
2 tablespoons ground
    almonds
2 tablespoons whey protein
    powder (vanilla or
    chocolate)
1 cup ice

1. In a small glass bowl melt the chocolate and agave in the microwave for approximately 20 seconds, then set aside.
2. Combine the cocoa with a little of the milk to make a paste then mix it with all the remaining ingredients. Place mixture into a blender or a large jug and, using a stick blender, blend until smooth.
3. Spoon a little melted chocolate into your serving glasses. Use the back of a spoon to spread around the inside of the glass.
4. Pour the thick shake over and serve with a little grated chocolate.

Yum, this is a delicious treat to start the day. Drink it with a high protein, low-carb breakfast such as an omelette.

High Protein Iced Espresso Coffee Ripple

SERVES 4

60g (2oz) whey protein
 powder (vanilla flavor)
1.2 litres (2pints) almond
 milk
80g (3oz) silken tofu
2 egg whites
2 tablespoons agave nectar
4 shots black espresso coffee
½ teaspoon ground
 cinnamon
4 large cups ice

1. In a large jug place the protein powder, almond milk, tofu
 and egg white with the agave nectar. Using a stick blender
 combine well together for 1 minute until very smooth.
2. Fill serving glasses with ice. Pour the milk mixture over the ice
 to almost fill the glass.
3. Make espresso or fresh pressed coffee and allow it to cool
 slightly, then pour over the top and serve immediately.

Strawberry, Cucumber & Orange Cooler with Mint Ice

SERVES 4-6

1 bunch mint, small leaves picked
120ml (4fl oz) cranberry juice
120ml (4fl oz) apple juice
750ml (24fl oz) water
8 strawberries, hulled and sliced
2 large cucumbers
2 oranges sliced
agave syrup to taste
1 lemon, finely sliced

1. Place one mint leaf into each cube of an ice cube tray and cover with water; freeze until completely frozen.
2. Blend juices and water with half of the strawberries, one peeled cucumber and one peeled orange. Strain through a fine sieve to remove excess pulp. Taste and adjust sweetness with the agave syrup. Refrigerate until ready to serve.
3. To serve, finely slice remaining cucumber and orange and place into a large jug with the strawberries, lemon and remaining mint. Add the ice cubes and pour over cooler, stir well and serve.

A cool refreshing drink, to enjoy in moderation.

Fresh Vegetable Juice

SERVES 4

4 celery stalks
2 large carrots
2 green apples
2 medium-sized beetroot
30g (1oz) fresh ginger
GARNISH
1 orange, peeled and sliced
½ small cucumber, thinly
    sliced
4 large strawberries
2 cups ice
4 sprigs fresh mint

1. Prepare your glasses by placing some of the sliced orange, cucumber and fresh strawberries with the ice in the bottom of the glasses.
2. Wash all vegetables well. Just before serving, pass all vegetables and fruit through a juicer, pour into a jug and stir together.
3. Pour the juice into the prepared glasses and serve with a sprig of mint.

Strawberry Mojito, Basil, Lime & Ginger

SERVES 4

½ punnet large ripe
    strawberries
2 fresh limes, cut into
    wedges
1 small knob of fresh ginger,
    finely grated
4 teaspoons agave nectar
600ml (1 pint) ice
600ml (1 pint) sparkling
    mineral or soda water or
    diet lemonade
8 leaves fresh green basil
8 leaves fresh garden mint

1. Trim stalks from the strawberries and cut into quarters. Divide the limes, grated ginger and strawberries equally between your 4 large glasses. Add a teaspoon of agave nectar and one basil and mint leaf to each glass.
2. Using a muddling stick, or the handle of a wooden spoon crush ingredients together for a minute or two until combined and fragrant.
3. Fill the 4 glasses with ice, top up with the sparkling mineral water and stir using a long cocktail spoon.

Tip: Swap with different berries when they are in season.

Get Up & Go Mango

SERVES 4

8 fresh raspberries
2 tablespoons agave nectar
1 large fresh ripe mango
1 small ripe banana
240g (8oz) natural plain
  yogurt
120g (4oz) silken tofu
600ml (1 pint) low-fat milk
100ml (3½fl oz) fresh orange
  juice
1 cup ice

1. Place raspberries and one tablespoon of agave nectar into a small bowl and mash with a fork until broken down. Set aside until serving.
2. Cut mango in half and remove flesh and skin from both halves. Place the mango with remaining ingredients into a blender and blend for 1 minute until smooth and thick.
3. Place a spoon of the fresh raspberry mixture into each glass and pour the mango liquid on top.

A perfect early morning treat before a good walk.

Banana & Berry Iced Smoothie

SERVES 4-6

3 large ripe bananas, peeled
   and sliced
juice and zest of ½ lemon
1 tablespoon agave syrup
250g (8oz) non-fat natural
   yogurt
240ml (8fl oz) low-fat milk
55g (2oz) bran
1 punnet (150g/5oz)
   raspberries

1. Blend bananas with lemon, agave, yogurt, milk and bran until smooth. Pour into a deep dish. Cover with plastic wrap and freeze until semi-frozen for about 2 hours.
2. To serve, spoon balls of banana mixture and layer in tall glasses. Top with fresh raspberries; serve immediately.

This is an iced breakfast treat. Use ripe fruit.

Homemade Baked Beans, Poached Eggs & Ham

SERVES 4

400g (14oz) dried haricot
   beans
olive oil
1 onion, finely chopped
2 cloves of garlic, crushed
2 celery sticks, chopped
1 teaspoon mustard powder
pinch cayenne pepper
200g (7oz) bottled tomato
   sauce (passata)
2 tablespoons cider vinegar
2 long green chillies, seeds
   removed and chopped

TO SERVE
poached eggs
toast
ham

1. Cover and soak beans in cold water overnight. Drain, rinse and drain again.
2. Heat oil in a large casserole dish and cook onion, garlic and celery over medium heat until softened. Add remaining ingredients. Add the soaked beans and mix well.
3. Add enough water to cover the beans. Place the lid on and simmer for 2½–3 hours over a low heat, or until beans are tender and sauce has reduced and thickened.
4. Serve beans on the side with poached eggs on toast with ham optional.

42

Beans are perfect for protein balance.

Apple & Pear Paste

MAKES 1 MEDIUM-SIZED JAR

4 ripe pears
4 red apples
2 tablespoons agave syrup
½ teaspoon vanilla-bean paste
125ml (4fl oz) pear nectar juice

1. Preheat oven to 160°C (320°F).
2. Peel, core and dice pears and apples and place into a large baking dish. Add agave and vanilla paste; pour over nectar.
3. Bake in oven, uncovered, for 1 hour. Stir occasionally while baking.
4. Remove from the oven and place apple and pears into a large saucepan. Mash fruit lightly with the back of a fork, bring to the boil and continue cooking until fruit has reduced and thickened.
5. Spoon into a dish and allow to cool.
6. Place in a jar with a seal-tight lid. This can be kept in the fridge for up to 2 weeks.

44

This is my own alternative to jam. Just a small amount on toast is like a reward to me. I spread cream cheese on first.

Orange Marmalade

MAKES 1 MEDIUM SIZED JAR

3 large oranges, sliced with
    skin on
30ml (1fl oz) honey
60ml (2fl oz) agave syrup

1. Place oranges into a medium saucepan and add enough water to come half way up the side of the pan. Cover and bring to a simmer. Cook for 10 minutes or until orange slices have softened.
2. Drain and discard any juices. Return orange to the same pan. Add honey and agave and stir to coat.
3. Cook over a very low heat for 1 hour, stirring occasionally. The oranges should begin to fall apart and the marmalade will thicken slightly.
4. Remove and cool. Cover and refrigerate until ready to serve. This can be kept in the fridge for up to two weeks.

This is not technically marmalade. Enjoy this in small amounts with low-fat ricotta or cream cheese on toast.

My Simple Figs on Toast with Ricotta

SERVES 4

4 slices of seeded bread
100g (3½oz) low-fat ricotta
2 ripe black figs (or
    fresh raspberries or
    strawberries)
1 teaspoon agave syrup

1. Toast the bread then mash the ricotta onto it using the back of a fork. Slice the figs and also mash them onto the ricotta.
2. Drizzle with a little agave syrup and enjoy with coffee or tea.

Replace butter with ricotta for a perfect snack.

Fluffy Lemon Ricotta Hotcakes

MAKES 8 HOTCAKES

2 large eggs
60g (2oz) stoneground flour
60g (2oz) bakers/self-
  raising flour
360ml (12.5fl oz) skim milk
½ teaspoon baking soda/
  bicarbonate of soda
240g (8.5oz) fresh ricotta
  cheese juice and zest of
  1 lemon
2 tablespoons agave nectar
2 tablespoons ground
  almonds
2 tablespoons flax seeds/
  linseeds
2 egg whites
confectioners'/icing sugar for
  dusting

1. In a small bowl whisk together whole eggs, flour, milk and bicarbonate of soda to form a batter the consistency of thick cream. In a separate bowl, whisk the egg whites to firm peaks and fold this into the batter.
2. In another small bowl, stir the ricotta, lemon zest and agave nectar together with the ground almonds and flax seeds.
3. Heat a medium-sized non-stick frying pan, spray with a little oil and add a large spoon of the batter to form a hotcake about 10cm (4in) across. Working quickly, add a tablespoon of the seed and ricotta mix to the hotcake.
4. Allow each hotcake to form bubbles on the surface and cook for 2 minutes then flip over and cook for another 2 minutes.
5. Serve hotcakes with a light dusting of sugar and a squeeze of fresh lemon.

Tip: Flax seeds are high in nutrients and Omega 3 and help lower the GI of the dish.

Lemon Chicken Schnitzel Sandwich

SERVES 4

2 chicken breast fillets
2 thick slices of day-old
   sourdough bread
2 tablespoons almond meal
2 teaspoons sesame seeds
2 tablespoons pumpkin
   seeds
2 tablespoons plain flour
1 egg, beaten
vegetable oil for shallow
   frying

MUSTARD MAYONNAISE
3 teaspoons Dijon mustard
55g (2oz) low-fat
   mayonnaise

TO SERVE
fresh sourdough rolls
salad leaves
sliced avocado
sliced tomato

1. Cut each chicken breast in half, slicing through the middle to make two thin fillets. Place between sheets of plastic wrap and pound lightly with a meat mallet to flatten slightly.
2. Remove crust from sourdough and process in a food processor until thin crumbs form. Add almond meal, sesame seeds and pumpkin seeds and pulse 1 to 2 times extra. Tip onto a flat plate or tray.
3. Dust chicken fillets in flour and dip into beaten egg. Crumb in bread/nut mixture. Heat a little oil in a non-stick skillet and cook fillets over medium heat until golden and cooked through. Drain on kitchen towel to absorb excess oil.
4. To make the rolls, mix mayonnaise and mustard together and spread over split rolls. Place avocado and sliced tomato followed by the chicken. Add extra salad to taste.

A sandwich can be a balanced meal.

Herb Roast Chicken Baguette with Ham & Roasted Tomato

SERVES 4-6

4 Roma tomatoes

salt and freshly ground black
  pepper

drizzle of extra virgin olive oil

4 whole-wheat baguette
  rolls, split

1 bunch rocket (arugula)

180g (6oz) cold green herb
  chicken

120g (4oz) shaved leg ham

1. Preheat oven to 180°C (350°F).
2. Halve tomatoes and place cut side up onto a cooking sheet. Season with salt and pepper and drizzle with a small amount of olive oil.
3. Roast in oven for 35–45 minutes. Tomatoes should be soft but still intact. Set aside to cool while building your sandwich.
4. Place rocket on the base of the roll and top with slices of cold chicken, followed by shaved ham. Cut cooled tomato halves in half again and place over the top of sandwich.

Look no butter! But the taste is delicious.

Olive Oil Eggs with Asparagus, Cheese & Jamon

SERVES 4

1 tablespoon olive oil

90g (3oz) olives, sliced with stones removed

4 large eggs

2 bunches asparagus, trimmed

90g (3oz) jamón, serrano or prosciutto (Spanish or Italian air-dried ham)

freshly ground sea salt and black pepper

120g (4oz) manchego cheese, shaved (or other hard sheep's milk cheese)

1. Warm oil and some of the olives in a non-stick skillet (frying pan) for 3 minutes. Carefully crack in eggs. Cook on a gentle heat until eggs are just cooked.
2. Cook asparagus in a pan of boiling salted water until just tender; drain and place on serving plate.
3. To serve, place the cooked eggs on top of the asparagus; place the ham around and scatter more of the olives over. Season with sea salt and black pepper. Top with shaved cheese.
4. Serve with some seeded crusty bread.

A great alternative for breakfast.

Mushroom, Pea & Bocconcini Omelette

SERVES 4

1 tablespoon olive oil
1 clove of garlic, crushed
120g (4oz) mushrooms,
    quartered
90g (3oz) fresh peas
3 egg whites, lightly beaten
2 egg yolks, lightly beaten
sea salt and freshly ground
    black pepper
4 baby bocconcini balls

1. Heat oil in a small non-stick skillet (frying pan) and cook garlic and mushrooms for 2–3 minutes. Add peas and cook for a further 2 minutes.
2. Carefully fold beaten egg whites and yolks together. Season with salt and pepper. Pour over mushrooms and peas and allow to set for 15 seconds on the bottom of the pan.
3. Drop bocconcini over the top and place directly under a hot grill (broiler) for 2 minutes, or until puffed up and cooked through.
4. Serve wedges with crusty sourdough or linseed bread.

A fantastic source of protein!

Pumpkin-Crusted Fish on Mash

SERVES 4

4 x 160g (5oz) sea bass
    fillets (or equivalent firm
    flesh fish)
1 medium-sized pumpkin,
    peeled and cut into cubes
1 orange, quartered with
    peel left on
sea salt and pepper
250g (9oz) non-fat natural
    yogurt
¼ bunch basil, leaves picked
    and shredded
80g (3oz) raw pumpkin
    seeds
cooking spray

1. Preheat oven to 180°C (350°F).
2. Place pumpkin and orange into a roasting dish and roast in the oven for 45 minutes, or until pumpkin is cooked. Remove half of the oranges and set aside.
3. Squeeze removed orange segments into the pumpkin and mash coarsely with a fork. Season with salt and pepper and set aside to keep warm.
4. Squeeze juice from remaining orange segments into yogurt and stir in basil. Season to taste.
5. Crush pumpkin seeds in a mortar and pestle until they have the consistency of coarse breadcrumbs.
6. Season the fish and press each fillet into the pumpkin seeds, ensuring it is evenly covered. Spray lightly with cooking spray and cook in a non-stick skillet (frying pan) for 2–3 minutes each side.
7. Serve the fish on the warm pumpkin mash with a spoon of the orange and basil yogurt.

Fish Burger with Lentil Dip & Cucumber Yogurt

SERVES 4

470g (1lb) firm white fish fillets (bass,
    snapper, monkfish), boned and skinless
2 egg whites
½ bunch coriander (cilantro), chopped
1 teaspoon harissa paste
pinch of salt

MOROCCAN LENTIL DIP
1 tablespoon olive oil
1 clove of garlic, crushed
1 teaspoon ground cumin seeds
1 teaspoon ground coriander seeds
pinch of ground fennel seeds
1 x 400g (14oz) can brown lentils, rinsed
    and drained
1 teaspoon brown sugar

CUCUMBER YOGURT
1 small cucumber, grated
250g (9oz) non-fat natural yogurt
juice of 1 lemon
¼ bunch mint, leaves picked and finely
    chopped

TO SERVE
wholemeal soy and linseed rolls and
    mixed leaves

1. Chill the fish and egg whites in the freezer for 15 minutes.
2. Using a blender process fish and harissa paste together until smooth. Add the egg whites and season with salt and pepper. Add the coriander (cilantro) and mix well. Divide mixture into 8 small patties and coat with cooking spray. Cook in a hot non-stick skillet (frying pan) for 3 minutes each side or until cooked, golden and firm to touch.
3. To make the Moroccan dip, cook garlic in oil for 1–2 minutes and stir in spices. Heat for a further 1 minute and add lentils, sugar and ¼ cup of water. Simmer for 10 minutes or until liquid has evaporated and lentils are thick. Cool slightly and process until smooth. Season with salt to taste and set aside.
4. Grate cucumber and squeeze out excess liquid; stir into yogurt along with lemon juice and mint.
5. To serve, place one slice of bread onto serving plates and top with 2 fish patties. Serve with a dollop of lentil dip and cucumber yogurt and mixed leaves.

Soft-Boiled Egg Dippers with Potato Hash & Salt Beef

SERVES 4

175g (6oz) piece brined
    beef silverside or brisket
¼ small white cabbage,
    finely shredded
sea salt and pepper
1 tablespoon white vinegar
½ medium onion
½ medium potato (Nicola)
½ medium sweet potato
30ml (1fl oz) vegetable oil
8 large eggs at room
    temperature
wholewheat toast to serve

1. Cook the silverside in a pot of lightly salted simmering water until tender for approximately 1 hour. Test by piercing with a small skewer. It should slide through the meat with no resistance. Remove from heat and allow beef to cool in the liquid. Once cool, use a fork to shred finely.
2. Meanwhile, cook the cabbage in a small pan just covered with cold water, a pinch of salt and the white vinegar. Bring to the boil and simmer until tender. Drain in a colander and set aside.
3. Using a coarse cheese grater shred the onion and potatoes into a bowl. Heat a medium-sized non-stick frying pan, add the vegetable oil and fry the potato and onion mixture for 10 minutes stirring frequently. Once the potato is tender add the drained cabbage and finely shredded salt beef. Continue to cook for a further 5 minutes.
4. Meanwhile, place eggs into a small pot of cold water and bring to the boil. Simmer for 4 minutes for runny eggs and 5 minutes for medium. Remove from the heat and place into egg cups for serving.
5. Cut the tops off the eggs and spoon as much of the cooked hash as you can onto each of them.

This is a great protein boost, especially for kids. The dish is also good with shaved ham or turkey.

Egg, Bacon & Mushroom Pita Pockets

SERVES 4

1 teaspoon olive oil

2 rashers bacon, shredded

1 medium-sized onion, finely
   chopped

175g (6oz) button
   mushrooms, sliced

8 large organic eggs

2 tablespoons light cream

sea salt and pepper

1 small knob butter

4 small wholewheat pita
   bread pockets or soft
   tacos

1. Heat a small non-stick frying pan, add olive oil and fry bacon
   with the onion for a few minutes. Add the sliced mushrooms
   and cook for 5 minutes until any liquid has evaporated.
   Cover and keep warm.

2. Crack the eggs into a small bowl, add the cream, sea salt
   and pepper and lightly whisk with a fork.

3. In another small non-stick frying pan add a small knob of
   butter, and as it begins to sizzle pour in the eggs and
   cook over a medium heat, stirring with a wooden spoon or
   spatula. Allow the eggs to settle in the pan and stir gently so
   they are creamy and scrambled.

4. Place the pita pockets in a medium oven 180°C (360°F) for
   approximately 3 minutes. Slice the top off each pita pocket
   and open them. Spoon in the scrambled egg mix and place
   the bacon and mushrooms on the top. If using soft tacos,
   warm them on a griddle pan first, fill with the scrambled
   eggs and bacon, then fold and serve.

Chickpea & Corn Fritters with Bacon & Avocado

MAKES 8 FRITTERS (2 PER PORTION)

1 medium brown onion
sea salt and pepper
4 rashers bacon
120g (4oz) fresh ricotta
3 eggs
175ml (6fl oz) milk (2% fat)
120g (4oz) stoneground
    wholemeal flour
½ teaspoon baking soda/
    bicarbonate of soda
300g (10oz) chickpeas/
    garbanzo beans, cooked
    washed and drained
175g (6oz) canned sweet
    corn kernels, drained
1 ripe avocado
½ lemon
1 tablespoon sumac (Middle
    Eastern) spice
30ml (1fl oz) vegetable oil

1. Preheat oven to 180°C (350°F). Peel the onion and cut into 8 wedges, drizzle with a little oil then season with sea salt and pepper. Cook in the oven for 20 minutes until soft and golden. Remove from oven and sprinkle with sumac spices. Keep warm.
2. Grill the bacon in a hot pan or on a barbecue plate until crispy.
3. In a small bowl mix the ricotta with a small whisk until smooth. Add the eggs and milk and whisk together briskly. Gradually add the flour and bicarbonate of soda to form a batter; it should be quite thick.
4. Roughly chop half of the chickpeas and mix both the chopped and whole chickpeas into the batter. Add the corn to the batter and season with a pinch of salt and pepper.
5. In another bowl mash the avocado with the back of a fork until broken down, season with sea salt and pepper and juice of half a lemon.
6. Heat a small non-stick frying pan, spray with a little oil and spoon in the batter. Add small fritters, approximately 8cm (3in) in diameter, and cook over a medium heat for 3–4 minutes each side.
7. Serve on a warm plate with the avocado, the roasted onions and the hot rashers of bacon.

68

This is a filling and nourishing breakfast. I often cook fritters in advance and pop them into the kids' lunch box.

Protein Boost, Scrambled Eggs with Tomatoes

SERVES 4

8 ripe Roma tomatoes
sea salt and pepper
1 clove fresh garlic, crushed
1 medium red chili, finely
  chopped
½ teaspoon superfine/caster
  sugar
8 large eggs
4 egg whites
80g (3oz) silken tofu
2 tablespoons olive oil
½ bunch fresh basil
grainy bread, toasted, to
  serve

1. Preheat oven to 180°C (350°F). Halve the tomatoes lengthways and place onto a baking tray. Brush with half the olive oil, then season with sea salt and pepper.
2. Spread tomatoes with the crushed garlic and chopped chili, then dust lightly with caster sugar.
3. Place onto a tray and roast in oven for 25–35 minutes.
4. Meanwhile, in a mixing bowl place the whole eggs, egg whites and tofu; whisk well together and season with sea salt and pepper.
5. Heat a medium-sized non-stick frying pan over a high heat, add the remaining olive oil. Add the fresh basil leaves and cook for 10 seconds. Add the eggs and tofu mixture, leave to cook for 10 seconds without stirring and, using chopsticks or a wooden spoon, gradually stir the eggs from the outside of the pan to the centre.
6. Once eggs and tofu become creamy, remove from the heat. The scrambled eggs should be undercooked and slightly liquid, however, the eggs will continue to cook in the pan. Serve on grainy toasted bread with the roasted tomatoes.

Hot Smoked Salmon &
Sweet Potato Omelette

SERVES 4

2 medium-sized sweet
    potatoes
sea salt and pepper
60g (2oz) butter
½ bunch continental parsley,
    chopped
juice of ½ lemon, plus extra
    to serve
300g (10oz) hot smoked
    salmon
    or ocean trout
6 large eggs
6 egg whites
30ml (1fl oz) olive oil
optional sourdough or
    wholegrain bread, toasted

1. Wash and peel the sweet potato and, using a coarse cheese grater, grate into a bowl. Season with a little salt and pepper.
2. Heat a medium-sized non-stick pan, melt the butter and add the sweet potato. Cook slowly over a medium heat for 10 minutes until soft and cooked through. Stir in the chopped parsley and a squeeze of the lemon juice.
3. Pick through the smoked salmon to remove any skin or small bones. Using your fingers, flake salmon into a bowl. Set aside.
4. In a separate bowl, mix the whole eggs and egg whites thoroughly, add a pinch of sea salt and some fresh ground pepper.
5. Heat a small non-stick frying pan and spray or wipe with a small amount of olive oil on a paper towel. Add a ladle of the egg mix to the pan and cook to form each omelette. Add some of the hot sweet potato mixture to the centre of the omelette and flake some of the salmon on the top.
6. Using the back of a fork flip half over and roll into a tube. Place each omelette onto a serving plate and serve with lemon wedges or slices and toasted grainy or sourdough bread.

73

This is full of flavor and goodness, and being low GI, it will fill you up. For me it's a win all round!

Sweet Potato Frittata

SERVES 4

2 medium sweet potatoes
1 tablespoon agave nectar
olive oil spray
1 tablespoon olive oil
1 red/Spanish onion, finely
    diced
1 clove garlic, crushed
2 rashers bacon, diced
4 large eggs
120g (4oz) silken tofu
2 tablespoons light cream
sea salt and pepper
¼ bunch flat parsley,
    chopped
4 egg whites
tomato or spinach salad, to
    serve

1. Preheat oven to 180°C (360°F). Peel and slice the sweet potato into discs approximately ½cm (¼in) thick. Brush with the agave nectar, and spray with a little olive oil. Place on a roasting tray and bake for approximately 25 minutes until soft, cooked and golden.
2. In a small non-stick frying pan heat the oil and fry the onion, garlic and bacon together for 3 or 4 minutes. Meanwhile, line ramekins or muffin moulds with some baking parchment and spray with olive oil spray.
3. In a small bowl whisk the eggs with the tofu and cream, season with salt and pepper. Add the chopped parsley.
4. Season the inside of the moulds with salt and pepper and alternately layer the bacon mixture and sweet potato slices until almost full. Pour the egg mixture over, making sure it covers the filling.
5. Place on a baking tray and bake in the oven for 20 minutes. Test with a small knife or skewer to make sure egg is just cooked in the middle.
6. Remove from oven and allow to cool before serving with a tomato or spinach salad. Also delicious served cold.

I use a non-stick individual muffin pan for this recipe, but small ramekins or moulds work just as well. They're great for school lunch boxes or fishing trips!

Baked Chili Eggs with Chickpeas, Spinach & Shaved Ham

SERVES 4

2 tablespoons olive oil
1 medium onion, finely diced
1 clove garlic
pinch smoked paprika
½ teaspoon dried chili flakes
4 ripe tomatoes, chopped
300g (10oz) can of organic
   chickpeas/garbanzo
   beans
sea salt and pepper
360g (13oz) fresh spinach
   leaves
8 large eggs
175g (6oz) finely shaved
   smoked ham
grainy bread, toasted,
   optional to serve
   (not included in carb
   exchange)

1. Preheat oven to 180°C (360°F). In a medium-sized non-stick frying pan heat one tablespoon of the olive oil and fry together the onion and garlic until light brown. Add a pinch of the paprika, chili flakes and the chopped tomatoes. Cook on a low heat for 15 minutes until a rich sauce has formed.
2. Add the chickpeas and cook a further 20 minutes. Season with sea salt and fresh pepper, and add more chili to taste.
3. In 4 small ovenproof dishes or ramekins, divide the spinach leaves and spoon over the hot tomato chickpea mix. Using the back of a serving spoon make a well on the top. Crack two eggs into each well. If you like your eggs really spicy, sprinkle some chili flakes or fresh chili on the eggs at this point.
4. Drizzle the top with a few drops of olive oil and bake for approximately 12 minutes until the eggs are cooked to your liking. Place shaved ham on the top and serve with some hot grainy bread, toasted.

The paprika and chili will stimulate your metabolism and get your body moving—it's a perfect spicy kickstart to your day.

Angel Hair Pasta with Salmon & Chilli Lime Dressing

SERVES 4

4 x 180g (6oz) salmon fillet,
    skin on
sea salt
3 tablespoons olive oil
2 limes, zest and juice
1 tablespoon agave syrup
1 long red chilli, seeds
    removed and finely
    shredded
2 kaffir lime leaves, finely
    shredded
80g (3oz) angel hair pasta

1. Rub both sides of salmon fillets with a little sea salt and some olive oil. Cook in a heated non-stick frying pan for 1–2 minutes each side, leaving salmon rare.
2. Mix lime zest, juice, agave, chilli and kaffir lime leaves together, then whisk in the remaining olive oil.
3. Cook pasta in a large pan of boiling salted water until al dente. Drain well and rinse under cold water. Drain again, place into a bowl and mix through the chilli and lime dressing.
4. Spoon pasta onto plates and serve with salmon.

BBQ Chicken with Red Quinoa Tabouleh Salad

SERVES 4

BBQ Chicken
1 clove garlic, crushed
30ml (1fl oz) olive oil
1 lemon, zest and juice
4 deboned chicken thigh fillets

DRESSING
1 lemon, zest and juice
1 teaspoon tahini paste
60ml (2fl oz) olive oil

SALAD
2 bunches flat-leaf parsley,
    leaves picked and washed,
    finely chopped
1 bunch fresh mint, leaves
    picked and washed, finely
    chopped
1 red onion, finely diced
sea salt and pepper
½ teaspoon sumac (Middle
    Eastern spice)
1 medium-sized Lebanese
    cucumber (¼ in/1 cm dice
    with skin on)
250g (9oz) cooked red quinoa
125g (4oz) natural yogurt

1. Marinate the Chicken by mixing together the garlic, olive oil and lemon zest and juice and brushing it onto the chicken thighs. Leave the chicken to marinate for 2 hours.
2. In a small bowl, whisk together the dressing ingredients.
3. Place the chicken thighs onto a hot barbecue or grill plate and cook for approximately 3–4 minutes each side until cooked through. Remove and allow to rest for a few minutes
4. In a large serving bowl, combine the parsley, mint and diced red onion. Season with sea salt, pepper and the sumac.
5. Carefully mix the cucumber and cooked red quinoa through the salad, dressing it as you go.
6. To serve shred the chicken and place onto the plates. Add a large spoonful of salad and drizzle with a little natural yogurt.

Fresh and light, this tabouleh salad has many uses

Tuna, Green Bean, Peanut & Mint Salad

SERVES 4

360g (12oz) fresh tuna fillet
olive oil
sea salt and pepper
120g (4oz) snake beans or
   green beans, finely sliced
400g (14oz) fresh bean
   shoots
2 small green zucchini/
   courgette, finely sliced
1 lemon, zest and juice
250g (9oz) cooked red
   quinoa
1 bunch fresh mint, picked
   leaves

DRESSING
80g (3oz) salted roasted
   peanuts
30ml (1fl oz) olive oil
pinch chilli flakes
2 tablespoons hot water

1. Rub the fresh tuna fillet with a little olive oil and season with sea salt and pepper.
2. Reheat a non-stick frying pan and sear the tuna on each side over a high heat for 1 minute. Allow to cool at room temperature.
3. In a small pot of boiling salted water, blanch the sliced green beans for 1 minute then refresh under cold water or in ice. Drain until required.
4. Make the dressing by crushing the peanuts in a mortar and pestle. Stir in the olive oil and chilli flakes. Adjust the thickness with some hot water.
5. In a large mixing bowl, place the beans, bean shoots and the sliced zucchini. Stir in the lemon zest and juice.
6. Add the cooked red quinoa then flake the tuna into the salad. Add the picked mint leaves and dress with the peanut dressing. Mix the salad together carefully, using a spoon.

This is a great salad as a main course or even as part of a brunch.

Turkey Club Sandwich

MAKES 4 LARGE SANDWICHES

1 small red/Spanish onion,
    finely chopped
½ clove garlic, crushed
2 avocados
sea salt and pepper
1 lemon
1 tablespoon olive oil
4 rashers bacon
8 thin slices of seeded
    sourdough or soy and
    linseed bread
60g (2oz) butter
240g (8oz) shaved turkey
    breast
8 slices reduced fat Swiss-
    style cheese
4 large eggs
½ iceberg lettuce, finely
    shredded
2 tablespoons low-fat
    mayonnaise
sweet potato fries, optional
    to serve

84

1. Preheat oven to 180°C (360°F).
2. In a mortar and pestle, place the red onions, garlic and avocado, and pound to a rough paste as for a guacamole. Season with sea salt and pepper and a squeeze of lemon juice.
3. In a large non-stick frying pan heat the oil, add bacon and cook for 2 minutes. Place on paper towels to drain.
4. Toast half the bread in a toaster or under a hot grill, spread with butter and place on a baking tray.
5. Spread toast with a spoonful of avocado mix then layer on shaved turkey and a rasher of bacon. Top with cheese slice and place in hot oven.
6. Meanwhile, using the same pan and oil the bacon was cooked in, fry the eggs and drain any excess oil, using kitchen paper. Toast the remaining bread slices.
7. Once the cheese is melting over the bacon, remove sandwiches from the oven. Place shredded lettuce on the cheese and a dollop of mayonnaise. Place egg on mayonnaise and top with buttered toast. Skewer each side of the sandwich with small wooden skewers and cut into strips or wedges as you like.
8. Serve with sweet potato fries and tomato dipping sauce.

This is my favorite sandwich—high in protein and delicious.

Hot Smoked Salmon, Potato, Lettuce & Dill Tip Salad

SERVES 4

2 slices soy and linseed
   bread
3 small chat potatoes
2 small cos lettuces
300g (12 oz) hot smoked
   salmon fillet
½ bunch dill tips
Dressing
½ bunch dill tips
125g (4oz) low-fat yogurt
1 tablespoon low-fat
   mayonnaise
zest and juice of 1 lime
sea salt and pepper
1 tablespoon olive oil

1. Cut the soy and linseed bread into small croutons and toast in a medium oven for 8 minutes until light brown and crisp. Allow to cool.
2. In a small bowl combine all the dressing ingredients together.
3. Cook the chat potatoes in salted water until soft and tender, keep warm.
4. Wash and trim the cos lettuce leaves then pat dry with a paper towel.
5. Prepare your serving bowls by arranging the salad leaves in them. Flake the salmon fillet over and cut the potatoes, sprinkle the croutons on the top and drizzle with the dressing.
6. Season and serve immediately.

Tip: Hot smoked salmon fillets are available at most good delis. It will look like it is already cooked, because it is.

I love this simple salad—it's crisp, light and really tasty with classic flavors.

Plank-Roasted Salmon with Quinoa Tzatziki

SERVES 6

1 side or large fillet of
    salmon
½ clove garlic, crushed
sea salt and pepper
30ml (1fl oz) olive oil
½ bunch flat-leaf parsley,
    roughly chopped
1 lemon, very thinly sliced
    with skin
1 loaf sourdough bread (not
    included in carb count)
    (optional, to serve)

TZATZIKI
1 small cucumber
sea salt and freshly ground
    black pepper
1 bunch fresh mint
½ clove garlic, crushed
250ml (9fl oz) natural Greek-
    style yogurt
½ lemon, juice and zest
250g (9oz) cooked white
    quinoa
pinch sumac (Middle Eastern
    spice)

1. Preheat the oven to 180°C (350°F).
2. Carefully check all pin bones have been removed from the salmon fillet. Lay the salmon skin-side down onto an untreated cedar plank, rub with the garlic then season with sea salt and plenty of black pepper. Rub with the olive oil. Sprinkle the parsley onto the salmon and cover with the thin slices of lemon.
3. Place the salmon on the plank into the oven for 8–12 minutes or until cooked how you like it.
4. To make the tzatziki, cut the cucumber in half, scrape out the seeds then grate the cucumber, with the skin on. Place this into a small bowl and season with sea salt. Leave it to stand for 30 minutes then drain all the liquid away.
5. With a sharp knife, finely shred the mint leaves and mix with the cucumber, crushed garlic and yogurt in a large bowl. Season with the zest and juice of the lemon and freshly ground black pepper. Stir in the quinoa and sumac and mix well.
6. Serve the bowl of tzatziki with the warm salmon on the board with some hot fresh bread.
7. Chef's note: Make sure that you use untreated cedar for your plank. You can purchase this from your local hardware store and cut it to size to fit in your oven. It will burn or smoke a little in the oven but that's fine—the smoke will impart a beautiful flavor to the salmon.

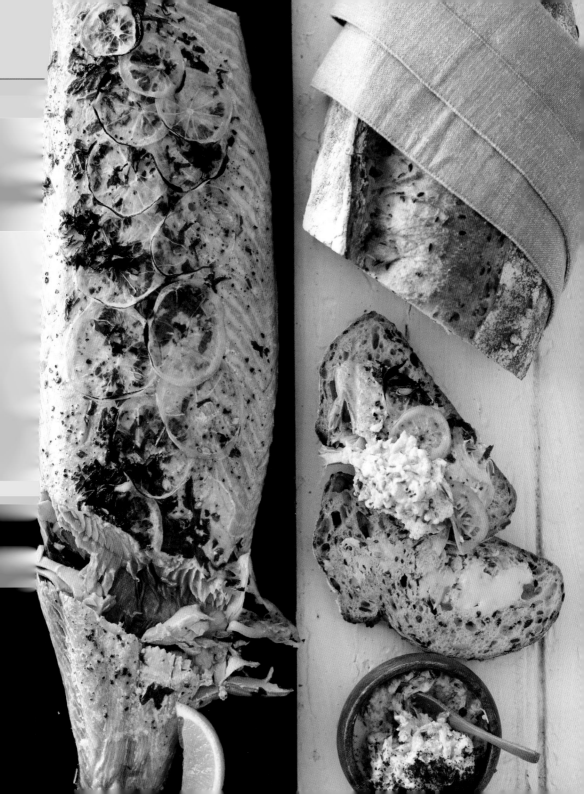

Steamed Fish Fillet with Baby Spinach & Dukkah Eggs

SERVES 4

4 x 120g (4oz) firm fish fillets
(snapper, kingfish)
½ teaspoon sea salt flakes
½ teaspoon freshly ground
black pepper
360g (13oz) fresh baby
spinach
6 large fresh eggs (cooked
in shell for 5 minutes from
boiling)
dukkah spice mix
85g (3oz) ground hazelnuts
2 tablespoons sesame seeds
2 tablespoons ground cumin
1 tablespoon ground
coriander
1 tablespoon ground fennel
seeds
pinch ground nutmeg
pinch ground cloves

1. Preheat oven to 180°C (360°F). Mix all the dukkah spice ingredients together in a bowl and pour onto a baking sheet. Place in the oven for 6 minutes, mix through with a fork and allow to cool. Keep in an airtight jar for up to 2 weeks.
2. Place a bamboo steamer over a large pan of boiling water (or use an electric steamer if you prefer). Season the snapper fillets with sea salt and freshly ground black pepper and put them onto a small plate, or a piece of greased baking parchment.
3. Put the spinach into a small bowl and season with a pinch of sea salt.
4. Place the snapper into the steamer to cook. After 3 minutes place the spinach into the steamer and continue to cook both spinach and snapper for a further 3 minutes until cooked through and firm to touch. Allow fish to rest in the warm steamer.
5. Peel the boiled eggs and slice into wedges. Drain any excess water from the spinach. Arrange on a plate with the snapper and wedges of egg. Sprinkle with plenty of the dukkah and serve.

The combination of ingredients makes this Angela's personal favorite and most requested dish for me to make at home!

Spice-Crusted Skillet Fish with Walnut Pesto

SERVES 4

4 x 120g (4oz) fish fillets
(kingfish, salmon, snapper
or tuna)
60g (2oz) low-fat feta cheese
Spice crust
1 tablespoon cumin seeds
1 tablespoon fennel seeds
½ teaspoon dried chili flakes
½ teaspoon smoked paprika
pepper
2 tablespoon olive oil
Walnut pesto
80g (3oz) walnut pieces
1 tablespoon pine nuts
1 medium red/Spanish
onion, finely diced
2 cloves garlic, chopped
2 tablespoons olive oil
1 tablespoon parmesan
cheese
1 sprig lemon thyme
2 tablespoons red wine
vinegar (good quality)
sea salt and pepper

1. For spice crust, use a mortar and pestle to grind spices together with the oil. Rub onto fish fillets, cover with plastic wrap and rest for 1 hour in the fridge.

2. Place the walnut pieces and the pine nuts onto a roasting tray and cook in a medium oven at 180°C (360°F) until lightly browned and toasted.

3. Preheat a small non-stick frying pan and fry the onion and garlic in the olive oil until softened. Allow to cool.

4. In a blender, mix the walnuts with the cooked onion, garlic, lemon thyme and parmesan cheese. Add the red wine vinegar and pulse to a pesto texture.

5. Preheat a heavy skillet or frypan, and cook the spice-crusted fish for 2 minutes on each side, allowing the spices to caramelise. Serve with some of the walnut pesto.

93

Walnuts are high in protein and fibre. The spices cook at the same time as the fish, which adds great flavor.

Rare Beef, Tuna & Green Bean Salad with Manchego & Capers

SERVES 4

120g (4oz) tuna fillet (fresh, or canned in spring water)
sea salt and pepper
240g (8oz) centre cut beef fillet
1 tablespoon olive oil
110g (4oz) low-fat mayonnaise
1 clove garlic
1 lemon
120g (4oz) green beans
60g (2oz) Manchego or parmesan cheese
1 tablespoon baby capers
lemon wedges, to serve

1. Preheat oven to 180°C (360°F). If the tuna is fresh, season it with some salt and pepper. Heat a small non-stick frying pan over a high heat and cook tuna for 1 minute each side, leaving the middle pink. Allow to rest and to cool, then flake it into a small bowl using a table fork. If you are using canned tuna, drain and place the tuna into a small bowl.

2. Season the beef fillet and cook in a hot non-stick frying pan with a little olive oil for 2 minutes each side to seal it, making sure to turn onto all sides.

3. Place beef on a baking tray and cook in oven for approximately 5 minutes. Try to leave it rare, then set aside to rest and cool for 5 minutes.

4. Meanwhile, combine the mayonnaise with the tuna, season with salt and pepper, finely grate a small amount of the garlic and some lemon zest into the bowl with the tuna and mix well.

5. Trim the ends from the green beans and blanch in boiling salted water for 1 minute then refresh in iced water until cold. Slice the beans thinly lengthways.

6. To serve, slice the beef as thinly as possible and place onto serving plates. Add a spoon of the tuna and arrange the green beans on the top. Shave or grate the cheese over the top and sprinkle a few capers around. Drizzle with a small amount of olive oil and serve with a wedge of lemon.

Cold Set Chicken Pasta Salad

SERVES 4–6

1 medium-sized whole fresh
    chicken (I prefer organic)
1 onion
1 stalk celery
2 fresh bay leaves
8 black peppercorns
120g (4oz) wholemeal spiral
    or penne pasta
1 small jar of marinated
    artichokes (cut in quarters)
2 tablespoons whole
    almonds, finely chopped

DRESSING
2 tablespoons low-fat Greek
    style yogurt
2 tablespoons low-fat
    mayonnaise
zest and juice of 1 lemon
salt and pepper

1. Place the chicken into a large pot of salted water with the peeled onion, celery, bay leaves and peppercorns. Bring to the boil and simmer slowly for approximately 45 minutes.
2. Prepare a large bowl or pot (large enough for the whole chicken to fit into) full of iced water. Carefully remove the whole chicken from the pot and put it directly into the iced water and allow to cool completely.
3. Cook the pasta in salted water until al dente, and refresh under cold water. Allow to drain.
4. In a small bowl, mix the yogurt, low-fat mayonnaise and the zest and juice of one lemon. Season with salt and pepper.
5. Remove the skin from the chicken and pick the breast and leg meat from the frame, tearing in small pieces and placing into a bowl.
6. In a separate bowl, mix the pasta with the chicken and artichokes, sprinkle the almonds on the top and serve with the dressing on the side.

This method of cooking chicken creates the most flavorsome and moist cold chicken. It's ideal for any type of cold chicken dish, sandwich or salad.

Crusty Chicken Schnitzel

SERVES 4

2 tablespoons pepitas/
  pumpkin seeds
2 tablespoons sunflower
  seeds
2 tablespoons white sesame
  seeds
45g (1.5oz) almond meal
45g (1.5oz)wholemeal flour
sea salt and pepper
2 eggs
4 x 120g (4oz) skinless
  chicken breast fillets
2 tablespoons vegetable oil
  for shallow frying
green salad leaves, to serve
2 lemons, to serve

1. Place the pepitas and the sunflower seeds in a blender, add the almond meal and pulse together for a minute or two. Don't let the mix become too fine, I like to leave it crunchy. Add the sesame seeds and mix through, then pour mixture into a small flat bowl.
2. Place the flour into another small flat bowl and season with sea salt and pepper. Break the eggs into another small flat bowl add a tablespoon of water and lightly whisk with a fork.
3. Lay chicken breasts on a cutting board and slice through the centre to open them up. Using a large knife lightly batter the chicken breast fillets so they become flat.
4. Lightly coat the chicken breast fillets in the seasoned flour, then pass through the egg mixture and finally into the almond meal and seed mixture.
5. Preheat the vegetable oil in a non-stick frying pan and cook the chicken on each side, until crumbs are golden brown and crispy and chicken is cooked through. Remove from the pan and drain on a piece of kitchen paper. Serve with green salad and fresh cut lemon.

Crunchy Chicken Nuggets

SERVES 4

500g (1lb) chicken breast,
  skin removed
355ml (12fl oz) buttermilk
80g (3oz) wholewheat flour
sea salt and pepper
pinch paprika
240g (8oz) raw buckwheat
120g (4oz) ground almond
355ml (12fl oz) vegetable or
  canola oil, for frying
Dipping sauce
175g (6oz) light sour cream
1 bunch fresh chives,
  chopped
juice and zest of 1 lemon

1. Dice the chicken breast into 1in (3cm) pieces and set aside in the fridge.
2. Pour buttermilk into a small shallow bowl. Place the flour into a separate small shallow bowl and season with sea salt and a pinch of paprika. Place the raw buckwheat into a mortar and pestle and grind lightly to just crack the kernels. Mix the ground buckwheat and almonds together and place onto a plate.
3. Coat the chicken in the flour, dip into the buttermilk and finally coat with buckwheat and almond mixture, making sure each piece is coated well. Roll gently between your palms. Place each crumbed nugget onto a tray lined with piece of baking parchment and chill in the fridge until ready to cook and serve.
4. Meanwhile, in a small bowl, combine the sour cream with the chopped fresh chives and the zest and lemon juice.
5. In a deep saucepan or deep fryer, heat the oil to 175°C (345°F) and carefully deep fry the nuggets, for approximately 4 minutes. Remove from the oil onto a paper towel to drain. Serve hot with the sour cream dipping sauce.

I love deep fried chicken, and this lower GI version is a fantastic alternative to the fast food options. The buckwheat absorbs less oil than traditional breadcrumbs.

Moroccan-Spiced Pumpkin, Tomato & Quinoa Salad

SERVES 6

1 medium-sized kabocha
    squash/Japanese pumpkin
60 ml (2fl oz) olive oil
8 Roma tomatoes
1 medium red onion, finely
    diced
1 clove garlic, crushed
250g (9oz) cooked chickpeas
    (garbanzo beans)
250g (9oz) cooked black
    quinoa
250g (9oz) cooked red quinoa
sea salt and pepper
1 lime, zest and juice
1 bunch flat-leaf parsley
1 bunch fresh mint
1 bunch fresh coriander
    (cilantro)

SPICE MIX
1 tablespoon fennel seeds
1 tablespoon cumin seeds
1 tablespoon coriander seeds
1 teaspoon flaked sea salt

1. Preheat the oven to 160°C (320°F). Toast the spices in a small non-stick frying pan for 3 minutes. Pour them into a grinder and blend to a powder.

2. Using a large strong knife, cut the pumpkin in half vertically. Scrape out the seeds from the centre and discard. Rub the flesh of one half in a little olive oil and dust with a tablespoon of the spice mix. Place the oiled pumpkin half on a roasting tray with the open side facing up. Bake in the oven for approximately 1 hour 15 minutes until tender. Peel the remaining half of the pumpkin (about 900g/32 oz) and dice into approximately 2cm (¾ in) square pieces. Rub these with a little olive oil and place on a roasting tray. Roast for 1 hour until cooked.

3. Cut the Roma tomatoes in half and rub with some olive oil. Place on a roasting tray and dust with some of the spice mix. Roast in the oven for 45 minutes until cooked and colored.

4. In a large frying pan, heat some olive oil and fry the onion and garlic. After 2 minutes, add the remaining spice mixture and chickpeas. Roughly chop the roasted tomatoes and add to the pan with the diced roasted pumpkin. Stir in the black and red quinoa and cook everything together for 5 minutes. Remove from the heat and allow to cool. Season with sea salt and pepper and stir in the zest and juice of the lime.

5. To serve, spoon the mixture into the pumpkin half and dress with the picked fresh herbs

Upside-Down Apple & Pear Crunch

SERVES 8

90g (3oz) unsalted butter
60ml (2fl oz) agave syrup
1 teaspoon ground nutmeg
1 teaspoon ground ginger
1 teaspoon ground
  cinnamon
4 green apples, peeled,
  cored and cut into
  wedges
2 green pears, peeled,
  washed and cut into
  wedges

CRUNCH TOPPING
30g (1oz) unsalted butter
2 tablespoons agave syrup
2 tablespoons rolled barley
  oats
85g (3oz) cooked red
  quinoa
2 tablespoons almond meal
2 tablespoons sunflower
  seeds
2 tablespoons pepita/
  pumpkin seeds
2 tablespoons flax seeds
1 tablespoon pecan nuts,
  roughly chopped

1. Preheat the oven to 180°C (360°F).
2. In a non-stick frying pan, melt the butter, agave and spices together. Add the wedges of apple and pear and cook on a low heat for 45 minutes until the fruit is soft and caramelised.
3. In a small bowl, melt together the butter and agave for the crunch topping.
4. In a mixing bowl, combine the rest of the ingredients of the crunch topping and coat everything in the melted agave and butter mix.
5. Line a small pie dish with a piece of greased paper then pack the fruit in firmly. Sprinkle over the crunch topping then bake in the oven for 35 minutes.
6. Remove from the oven and allow to cool for 5 minutes before serving. Then carefully invert onto your serving plate.

Chef's note: Serve with a little light pouring cream or some agave ice cream.

Baked Strawberry, Lime & Quinoa Custard Pudding

SERVES 8

3 large fresh free range eggs
60ml (2fl oz) agave syrup
1 teaspoon vanilla paste
½ lime, zest and juice
2 tablespoons quinoa flour
250g (9oz) cooked white
  quinoa
250ml (9fl oz) cream
250ml (9fl oz) milk
500g (1lb) large fresh
  strawberries

1. Preheat the oven to 180°C (350°F).
2. Using an electric beater, whisk together the eggs with the agave syrup, vanilla paste and the lime zest and juice.
3. Whisk in the quinoa flour until combined then stir in the cooked white quinoa.
4. In a small pan, bring the cream and milk to a simmer then remove from the heat and allow to cool for 5 minutes.
5. Stirring constantly, pour the cream mixture over the egg mixture.
6. Trim the tops from the strawberries and arrange in a small baking pie dish with the tips facing up.
7. Carefully pour the quinoa custard around the strawberries, leaving the tips uncovered.
8. Bake in a preheated oven for 1 hour until custard is set and light brown in color.
9. Serve warm with some pouring cream or ice cream.

Baked Strawberry, Lime & Quinoa Custard Pudding

SERVES 8

3 large fresh free range eggs
60ml (2fl oz) agave syrup
1 teaspoon vanilla paste
½ lime, zest and juice
2 tablespoons quinoa flour
250g (9oz) cooked white
   quinoa
250ml (9fl oz) cream
250ml (9fl oz) milk
500g (1lb) large fresh
   strawberries

1. Preheat the oven to 180°C (350°F).
2. Using an electric beater, whisk together the eggs with the agave syrup, vanilla paste and the lime zest and juice.
3. Whisk in the quinoa flour until combined then stir in the cooked white quinoa.
4. In a small pan, bring the cream and milk to a simmer then remove from the heat and allow to cool for 5 minutes.
5. Stirring constantly, pour the cream mixture over the egg mixture.
6. Trim the tops from the strawberries and arrange in a small baking pie dish with the tips facing up.
7. Carefully pour the quinoa custard around the strawberries, leaving the tips uncovered.
8. Bake in a preheated oven for 1 hour until custard is set and light brown in color.
9. Serve warm with some pouring cream or ice cream.

Baked Strawberry, Lime & Quinoa Custard Pudding

SERVES 8

3 large fresh free range eggs
60ml (2fl oz) agave syrup
1 teaspoon vanilla paste
½ lime, zest and juice
2 tablespoons quinoa flour
250g (9oz) cooked white
    quinoa
250ml (9fl oz) cream
250ml (9fl oz) milk
500g (1lb) large fresh
    strawberries

1. Preheat the oven to 180°C (350°F).
2. Using an electric beater, whisk together the eggs with the agave syrup, vanilla paste and the lime zest and juice.
3. Whisk in the quinoa flour until combined then stir in the cooked white quinoa.
4. In a small pan, bring the cream and milk to a simmer then remove from the heat and allow to cool for 5 minutes.
5. Stirring constantly, pour the cream mixture over the egg mixture.
6. Trim the tops from the strawberries and arrange in a small baking pie dish with the tips facing up.
7. Carefully pour the quinoa custard around the strawberries, leaving the tips uncovered.
8. Bake in a preheated oven for 1 hour until custard is set and light brown in color.
9. Serve warm with some pouring cream or ice cream.

About the Author

With a career spanning almost three decades, Michael Moore is renowned for his work as a chef, author and TV presenter. He has cooked for some of the world's top celebrities and has become a household name on shows such as Fresh, Junior MasterChef and The Biggest Loser and appears on NBC's Today Show and New York's Morning News, reaching an audience of 29 million viewers.

Raised in England, Michael developed a love of cooking at an early age. It was while studying classical cookery at college that he developed his interest in the scientific aspects of food and nutrition that have come to set him apart from his peers today.

Five years ago, personal circumstances changed the trajectory of his career. He was already living with diabetes and for a top chef surrounded by great food, he faced the daily challenge of healthy eating. Then, one day out of the blue, he suffered a major stroke while out to dinner with his family, an event that changed his life forever.

It was this episode that inspired his best selling Blood Sugar cook book series; a collection of beautifully presented and inspiring recipes that break the mould in diabetic cooking.

'Being a diabetic doesn't mean you are stuck in a "gastronomic wilderness". You can enjoy great food that's unexpected and exciting whilst keeping your sugars under control', says Michael.

This healthy eating philosophy underpins the menus at his restaurant O Bar and Dining, located in Sydney's CBD. The food is an unexpected journey of contemporary dining with a healthy spin.

Michael is a committed charity Ambassador and supporter to The National Breast Cancer Foundation, The Sydney Children's Hospital Foundation, Starlight Children's Foundation, St. Vincent's Hospital Foundation and more recently, The Garvan Institute of Medical Reseach, National Stroke Foundation and Diabetes Australia.

Michael currently sits on Tourism Australia's Advisory Board as a culinary ambassador.

With his profile and brand continuing to build internationally as he spreads his message about healthy eating, this global entrepreneur is set to continue to reinvent the dining experience on both sides of the world.

Follow Michael Moore on social media:
Twitter – @michaelmooresyd
Facebook –www.facebook.com/ChefMichaelMoore

Twitter – @obardining
Facebook – www.facebook.com/Obardining
Instagram – @obardining
www.obardining.com.au

Index

First published in 2015 by New Holland Publishers Pty Ltd
London • Sydney • Auckland

www.newhollandpublishers.com

A record of this book is held at the British Library and the National Library of Australia.

ISBN 9781742578514

Managing Director: Fiona Schultz
Project Editor: Jessica McNamara
Designer: Lorena Susak
Production Director: Olga Dementiev
Printer: Toppan Leefung Printing Limited

10 9 8 7 6 5 4 3 2 1

Keep up with New Holland Publishers on Facebook
www.facebook.com/NewHollandPublishers